The Gift of Now

by Carmen Melissa Hall

Library of Congress Cataloging-in-Data
Hall, Carmen, 2017-The Gift of Now: Discovery of your purpose
2017917374
ISBN-13:978-1973706168
ISBN-10:1973706164

Foreword

We all have a voice, a mission, and a purpose. We are born with it. Uncovering these things is a process and something that takes time. Pieces of it come to light here and there and we learn to proclaim and whisper and shout out our voice, to live our purpose, and to fulfill our mission during the journey of our lifetime. During this journey we come across many people who season and influence our lives for good and for ill. People, who through their influence and experience, help us to discover who we are. They help us to uncover our direction, sometimes help us to establish our purpose, clarify our mission, and often to celebrate the beauty that is in us; they see our light and rejoice in it. Of course, at times, we come across people that, for the worse, suppress, oppress and hold us back, quiet us, and even shout us down; it is the way of the human creature to sometimes be this way. Just the same, it is always our hope that we find more of the former and less of the latter.

In my journey I have been blessed to find a friend and a woman of light whose voice sings a song of rejoicing, whose mission and purpose is to build up the people around her. She sees beauty, she shares light. This book you hold in your hands right now is part of her journey, part of her mission, being to share that light with others, with you, to help you in your journey to understand your intrinsic, unfathomable, timeless, immeasurable value.

Carmen and I go back many years to a much simpler time when she was still Missy and just a cute girl with a big, radiant smile. I was just a girl myself, trying to sort it all out as we all do when we are kids. Who to be friends with, who is kind, who is not, who to stay away from, who can be trusted, who is mean, who will laugh with you, who will laugh at you...you know how it is in junior high and high school...it's a rough place sometimes. It was these sometimes good, sometimes not-so-good hallways where I first met my friend Missy, now Carmen, and we became friends.

From the beginning Carmen was a sparkly-eyed, happy, smiling young woman. She was kind and loving to those around her, friendly, and sweet. Not once did I ever see her tear anyone down. She never said one mean word to me, one frowny face, one unkind thing. In fact, every time we interacted, it was just her beautiful, happy face, her laughing, and joyful words. She, in my history of teenage-dom, was a point of light. I'm sure she had her up days and down days just like we all do, her peaks and valleys, but as a rule, she has always been someone who has had a sweet heart, a sincere spirit and a desire to lift others up. She is a builder and not a destroyer, and so it has been that these things have not changed through the years.

After graduating high school, as it often happens, we lost touch. Not unusual, especially since she stayed local to the Cleveland, Ohio area and I did not. I moved back east and then out west. She walked her path, went to school and to work, establishing herself as a wife and mother, friend, church and community member, a working woman, mentor and writer—and most especially a builder of people. Likewise, I did many of these same things myself, things that would set the path for the rekindling of our friendship and understanding of one another.

"Friendship … is born at the moment when one person says to another "What! You too? I thought I was the only one."

As we have reacquainted ourselves with each other as adult women, we have found a renewed and delightful friendship. Our friendship, while rooted in our youth and the kindness found therein, has grown by the goodness and the strength that we see in each other as women of light who believe in growing and building the people around us.

Some of our most common points of belief are…

♣ The immeasurable potential of human beings.

♣ There is an intrinsic light that people hold within them.

♣ Humans are beautiful and extraordinary creatures that merit the time and the love and the effort to coax the potential that lies within.

♣ It is never too late to live a life. It is never too late to discover something new within. It is never too late to change and to grow, to develop and to become.

- ♣ We can all do hard, extraordinary things, if we will only believe it and just take that first step and try.
- ♣ Kindness, compassion, service and love can change the world if we will but do it.

Part of our shared purpose, our commonality that we live for, is to lift up those that sorrow, those that are weak and despairing, to help those that are suffering, or those that are seeking their way to greater joy and light. Part of our purpose is to share happiness. All of our purpose is to love.

> *"Wherefore lift up the hands which hang down, and the feeble knees;"*
> *—Hebrews 12:12*

As you move through the pages here with an open heart you will see that there is beauty all around, but especially that there is great potential and beauty that is within you. You are a creature of light! We both believe and know that you, and I, and she, and he, and we, are all wonderfully made! Her uplifting words of love, and hope and counsel, are for you. She has thought, and pondered, written, rewritten, prayed, and sought out inspiration, all with the purpose to build you up, to share her experiences and learnings in order to help you succeed, to help you find joy, to help you see your value and your purpose, to help you find your own mission, and your own voice.

Life is a journey, and a path, and we travel it one step at a time, one day at a time. Do you live it—your life—or is it merely something you wander through? Do you love it? Do you own it? Do you use your voice? Can you hear it? Where do you want to go? What do you want to do? What is your purpose, your mission? Who do you want to be?

As you read The Gift of Now, reflect, and dream. Ask yourself all the questions, and as you ponder on the answers, think about where you want to go next and where you want to go right now. Write in your book, highlight it, put your thoughts in the margins and in the empty spaces and pages, write your dreams and your desires, no matter how outlandish or out of reach they may seem. Own it all. Think it out. Now is a new day with a new opportunity to choose new things, new directions, new places to go.

You hold the power to change. It starts with you and it can start with the smallest of steps, and the tiniest of actions. Do one thing differently. Just one, and let the avalanche of change and joy follow. Choose your life. Live your life your way. Don't give your power of agency, decision and choice away to someone else. If your life is not what you want it to be, or you want more, or you want different, seek it out. Become the human being you desire most to be. Today, in this very moment, no matter how old you are, no matter where you are in your life, if you want to change, if you want to do something differently, if you want to make your life explode in light and joy and laughter, and in all of the ways that are most important to you, in all of the things that matter most, then go do those things. Go make those things happen.

You have great things in you to do. Believe it. You can do hard, amazing things. You've got this. Carmen believes in you, it's why she wrote this book. I believe in you, it's why I wrote this foreword. We believe it, because we believe in, and see it in, all the people in this human family over and over again, not just some of them, all of them—and you're part of all the people!

Find your joy. Find your purpose. Live with gusto and share your effervescent, glorious light.

The time is now. Get out there. Live. Be the person YOU have always wanted to be!

I wish you peace and light, and joyful discovery.

Tracy D. Zalit Davidson, PMP
People Builder, Believer in the Intrinsic Good
Salt Lake City, Utah
November 8, 2017

I was born to do what I do
I was conceived to be who I am
I am because He made me
Only I can do what I
Was put here to do
My only my voice can say
What needs to be heard from me
My very presence is necessary to make a change.
I am important, I am worth much,
I am to be valued
Because the Creator created me.

"My GIFT is a very special talent given to me from my Creator. My PASSION is the intensity and the level of energy that I go about demonstrating that "thing" that I love to do. My PURPOSE is the way that I exercise and utilize my gift to significantly impact the lives of others."
Carmen Melissa Hall

The moment when something on the inside of you is trying to breakthrough to do something that you had no clue that it would do for you or others, is the moment that you discover that there is a reason why you are here. Although everything may not be realized in that exact moment, there is enough power in that moment to provoke you to investigate what it is that you are being called to do.

For many years, I have known that there was a book that I was going to write. I have not always been sure about the content of the book, but I knew that I would be the author. As I am writing, I am feeling confident enough to embark on this unknown journey, however I am still unsure of the entirety of its content. But what I do believe is even though you don't know everything or can't see the big picture, this book will propel you to action, encourage you to step out on faith and follow the lead of the very thing that has been tugging at your soul. You will be compelled to move, to take the first step on your journey to fulfilling your purpose.

As I reflect, even in this very moment, I am reminded of my 4th grade teacher Mr. Noble. He taught me how to write book reports and from that point on, I was in love with English and writing. If I am being honest, I can't recall feeling that way about every English teacher or class, but I do know that is where my passion for writing all started. It wasn't until after I was married and had 4 of my 5 children did I return seriously to writing again. It was completely unexpected.

One day an entire song came to me. It caused me to stop what I was doing, find a pen and paper to hurry and write it all down. The song was pouring out of me like uncontrollable tears sometimes do. There were verses and a vamp, even a bridge and a hook, you songwriters will know what I'm talking about. If you know anything about the arrangements of a song, you will know that all of those things must not only be present but in harmony to bring a song to its completion. Anyway, I was a little shocked because I had never written a song before. I failed to mention that as I received the lyrics that were pouring out of my fingertips, there was a melody that flowed right along with it. That was my very first experience with writing a song. This also marked the beginning of my daily journaling. I would make certain that there was always a pen and paper, or whatever nearby to collect any random thoughts that were pertinent enough to write down.

My point in sharing that experience, is having the ability to recognize when a seed is planted in your life, and how that seed in that very moment brings you so much fulfillment that even when it is not practiced or utilized on a regular basis, somehow it finds a way to get your attention for a greater **purpose** later in life. I decided to accept and acknowledge writing as my gift. It ever so kindly showed up in my life in a way that I was not anticipating at all. I had not been thinking about writing anything. I was so preoccupied with four children, a husband and another child baking in the oven that I had no thought or seemingly time to write much less focus on writing. To say the least,

4

my gift surprised me when it showed up. I must say even in that moment, I was not aware that it was showing up to prepare me for the writing of this book. In many ways, writing was baking in the oven like my youngest child.

One day I had a vision or let me say that I am not quite sure what to call it exactly, but a picture popped up in my head of a book cover that looked like a beautifully wrapped gift with a soft flowing bow. I thought to myself 'this is a sign' and that whenever I write this book, that it would be called The Gift. I must say I was pleased with that title until sometime last year, in 2016 it was made very clear to me in another one of my random unexpected thoughts or visions as I call them, that it would be called THE GIFT of NOW. My spirit agreed with that thought immediately. Even as I write this book, there are many things that continue to be revealed to me about this book. The unveiling of thoughts, ideas, and purpose come forth readily and with such clarity.

My hope for all who read this book, is a stronger conviction and purpose, that you learn to not only listen but trust the voice inside of you that speaks to you, a quiet voice inside that won't be silenced but instead constantly tugs at your soul. A voice that continually gives you meaning, purpose, and life. My hope is that you pay close attention to the many confirmations that will come to you through words, sight, hearing, and people, those you know and those you have yet to encounter. My hope is that you don't ignore the constant tugging at your soul and stirring of your spirit but instead fearlessly investigate it, explore it and answer the call.

Ok so here we go.... I have a confession, I am not as avid a reader as I use to be when I was in elementary school but when I read books back then, I loved the way a book would have me so engaged that I felt like I was in the very presence of the characters, actually part of the book. I loved when I could feel the feelings of the people, their lives, and their stories. That's my goal for my writing, to keep you engaged as I continue to share this wonderful writing experience with you. My hope is to bring my writing to life so that you too can experience the feelings of recognizing and living your purpose.

So, I have decided to keep it as real as possible. I feel like I don't know where to start so I suggest we all get ready for the unwrapping of this (my) gift together and enjoy the winding journey we will take together as I share with you.

The Beginning

There is nothing quite like waking up and doing exactly what you know you are **purposed** to do. When I woke up today, I did my regular, to pray and thank the Most High God for waking me up. Somewhere in His infinite plan, He knew that this would be the day that I would no longer procrastinate on writing this book. I feel like I am one with the Universe as I am typing in this moment. I am no longer concerned with the content, but I am completely fulfilled with the action, the actual demonstration of proactively using the gift that He gave me. It did not cost me any money, nor did it cause me any hurt, harm or pain to simply put life to what He had already created in my heart and thoughts. There is a knowing, a feeling, and a connection in your spirit that occurs when you are operating in your **purpose**. A sense of unexplainable peace that encompass your being.

There were so many things that I thought that I needed to have to feel confirmed and validated as a writer, but that was not the case. When something is ordained for your life, you can't avoid it, run from it, hide from it or even qualify it. It just is! **Purpose** by its own definition, is being the reason for which something is done or created or for which something exists, confirms this fact. What I have found in the exploration of my purpose is that I didn't choose my purpose, it chose ME.

Ironically, the first song that I wrote, that I referenced at the beginning of this book is called He Chose Me. There is no better time than now to share with you those lyrics:

> *From the foundation of the earth, from the beginning of all time I have loved you with an everlasting love, I have drawn you with loving kindness sacrificed for sin so you can be my witnesses. Jesus you called me by my name in my mother's womb though undeserving and full of shame, Lord you redeemed me unto righteousness never belonging to myself or no one else... It took the renewing of my mind for me to finally realize that*

you chose me, You said if I abide in thee you too would also abide in me, You chose me... He chose me, anointed me for this appointed time, He chose me, anointed me for this appointed time...I am a chosen generation, a royal priesthood, You chose me...I am a holy nation a people for God's own possession, You chose me...He chose me, anointed me, for this appointed time...He chose me...(fades out)

That song by itself was a clear sign to me that this gift of mine is certainly much bigger than just me. It is a gift that is supposed to be shared, to offer healing, strength, courage, and faith to the world. It is selfish of me to hide my gift from others. After writing that song, I felt like my spirit was opened, like I had been given a key and unlocked what He had placed in me from the foundation of the earth. It is amazing how confirmation and validation simply arrive at the doorstep of your heart once you take the first step to doing what you are **purposed** to do. When the light switch is turned on, you definitely know it! The doubt that you once felt is no more. The power of being validated and confirmed in your purpose propels you further along on this journey to your destiny. Creating meaning within your life is the fulfillment of purpose.

My Gift
My gift is my way of escape
It is the success of my life
My gift is the conduit to my purpose
It is the satisfaction of my soul...

My Affirmation

To Serve, an act of performing a duty or services to or for another person(s). I know and accept that being of SERVICE to others is part of my **purpose** as well. I am choosing to be a vessel, to be used by the Most High God for His purpose. A purpose I believe is to reach as many people as possible and help them along on their journey. There is no greater gift than that which allows us to be used for His purpose. *I am purposed to be of service to others.*

Energy provides life, illuminates thought, and creates action. Recognizing the power of personal energy, I recognize my own power as an influencer of thought and action. I am cognizant of my role in creating positive illumination. I must live and conduct my life in a way that allows my gift to be an extension of that energy; to serve as a beacon of light that illuminates thought and creates action.

As a beacon of light, I am recognizing and acknowledging that it is through my light that I am being used in service for His purpose. My illuminating light serves as a guiding influence for those whose pathway I encounter. I shine brightly, sharing hope, providing direction, and helping others as they journey through life.

I know that when I enter a room the atmosphere must change. The energy of my light should be illuminating to those in my presence. It is understanding this responsibility that I have been given that I move seamlessly through the Universe. I admit, I am not immune to the chaos, trauma, drama, and adversity of everyday life. In those moments I am challenged to always remember my purpose, my obligation, my responsibility and through these experiences I have learned to continue to walk in my purpose. I acknowledge that there is something greater than I, a task to be fulfilled, and that is what keeps me focused on cultivating and nurturing my gift.

Whether we chose to own it or not, we have all been given an assignment. An assignment that requires us to use our gift. This assignment is the fulfilling of our purpose. The very foundation of our purpose is to be used by the Most High, to be of service to others. Service by its very nature is the act of surrender and the act of giving. How we chose to serve is directly related to the assignment we have been given. Once you have been assigned your gift there is nothing or no one person who can rescind it!

Wonderfully Made

There is a scripture in Psalms 139:13-16 that expresses the way in which we were all so carefully and uniquely created and the translation that I love so much is this: "For you formed my inward parts, you knitted me together in my mother's womb. I praise you, for I am fearfully and wonderfully made. Wonderful are your works; my soul knows it very well. My frame was not hidden from you, when I was being made in secret, intricately woven in the depths of the earth. Your eyes saw my unformed substance; in your book were written, every one of them, the days that were formed for me, when as yet there was none of them." (ESV Psalms 139:13-16) What amazes me most about this passage of scripture is that it clearly implies that no two of us are created the same. We were thought of with distinct intention. The purpose for your life is shared with no one else. It is identified just the same as your fingerprint. There is not another soul that can do what you were put here to do, in the way you are purposed to do it.

It is so important that we don't get lost in comparing ourselves to any other person. What we individually have to offer is just that, our own gift. We are all destined to express our own greatness. I believe that I am the evidence of God's greatness and that you are too. It is very human of us to compare ourselves to others, but it is not necessary. The sooner we trust in our gift and what we have to offer, the sooner the world gets to benefit from the creativity placed inside of each of us. The world is waiting on you! You already have everything you need on the inside of you to do what you've been called to do. No doubt, there will be obstacles, but those things only come to help you in your discovery and build strength and character. Your confidence will come with action. You are not to be compared, for you are wonderfully made.

Capturing Moments

If you know me, you know that being in front of and behind any camera is a place that I absolutely enjoy occupying. There is something magical about capturing moments that we seemingly will never get back. Sometimes our minds will fail us, but a picture takes that moment and holds it in time, right down to the second and no one can ever change the moment. When we are able to truly live in that precise moment, we are able to savor it, we are able to give it our undivided attention, and we are able to give to it the attention that it deserves. That is what gives value to the moment enjoyed. It can't be taken away or changed.

Live in each moment that you are graced with. Allow yourself to fully experience and appreciate the moment, the emotions, the thoughts, the feelings, the sensations...the moment. Even as I am writing this, I am thinking of how moments before, I didn't even know what I was going to be typing and because I stayed in the moment, this is my outcome.

Moments are a synopsis of the story we desire to tell. Learning to "be" in the moment is contrary to what we are taught. We are constantly looking ahead and behind, rarely do we look at the right now. Walking in purpose requires that we focus on the now. That we listen in the moment. We must learn to quiet our spirit and our minds to hear. When we do that we are able to focus more clearly on our gifts, our purpose for being.

We are extraordinary beings, yet we are faced with so many distractions that make every attempt to delay that which is meant to positively impact the lives of others. One major thing that I have learned is that distractions come to steal our joy in the moment. They are disruptors by design. They come to take us away from our purpose, to disrupt the journey towards fulfillment, to distract us in the moment from that which is being required of us. We have the choice to stay focused or be lead astray by things that have no real power.

Pause and Listen...

Many times, we have been in situations where we have received advice from our parents or elders, sometimes even our peers and we simply brush it off. Sometimes it goes in one ear and out of the other. But then someone comes along and offers that very same advice and your ears accept each and every syllable of what that person had to say. Part of the journey to discovering your purpose is taking the pause and listening. Sometimes in taking our pause we have moments of uncomfortable silence.

We live in a world where silence or stillness is the opposite of busyness. We have been conditioned to believe that if we are not making noise we are not accomplishing or being productive. Yet in the stillness, the silence, we are still working. Still being prepared. I believe that we have to first learn to become comfortable with the silence, so that we are able to hear with clarity what our next move should be. That is the importance of being obedient when you are moved to do or say something. I found that once I became comfortable with the silence, I was able to effectively hear what

I was supposed to do. Just as you were able to hear from another person being used as a vessel for you, your voice is the same for someone else. Your voice is where they need to get the motivation and encouragement to move forward.

...so my fingertips are listening to my heart and they are being obedient.....

As I continue to be obedient, my **purpose** is being fulfilled, even though I don't know what the end looks like, I continue to be still and sit in silence. I have no clue as to how this book will be published or how relevant it will be to anyone else's life at this moment, but what I do know is that I have shown up, my fingertips are listening to my heart and they are being obedient to this moment right now!

The only thing that your gift and my gift require of us is Obedience. The intent is for our gifts to be used to do something powerful and life changing for someone else. Our gifts may not bring us fame or recognition by the multitudes, but it will fulfill God's divine **purpose** that He has so graciously and freely bestowed upon us. What we don't want to do, is to leave this earth without fulfilling our specific assignment. Every day is a right now moment. We have to treat our gifts with respect and allow them to work to their fullest capacity. If we knew that our gifts would be a guaranteed avenue to monetary success, we would not procrastinate or hesitate to put it to use.

Our gifts should not be deterred by the daily events that occur in our lives but instead interwoven into the fabric of our being so that it becomes an extension of who and what we are. We must not overlook or neglect our gifts. We must always understand that there is someone or something waiting on what we have to offer. Each one of us has the potential to be a "change agent." In other words, we all have that something that can literally change someone else's life simply because of our obedience to the call.

What I am finding in this process of writing, is that the more mentally determined I am to get the book finished, the more procrastination and distractions. I honestly feel like there is a force that does not want it to get finished. That thought alone is the motivation for me to press on, move forward, and stay the course even more diligently. This leads me to the subject of operating and existing in your comfort zone.

Comfort Zones

*Familiar places, religious and
traditional acts, unchallenging, never
moving situations…should they
remain or should they depart? Life's
circumstances, life's tribulations, our
reactions always the same…why?
Comfort Zones…Feels good to your
flesh, spiritual growth-dormant. Fear
undiscovered, never knowing what's
on the other side. Comfort
Zones…Destiny denied? No, just
delayed…Why? Comfort Zones
Do you win or lose?
What will you choose?
Will you stay or will you trust God
and Go?*

This piece was a little something that I wrote in the early 2000's and its relevance is just being revealed to me NOW! This speaks to the importance of understanding that every moment has a **purpose** of its own. When you finally accept and believe what you are put here to do, it will literally force you out of your comfort zone.

Interestingly enough, I had an experience with my higher power about 10 years ago where I was sitting still in His presence and an overwhelming thought came to my mind, "I am a writer." I felt compelled to say it out loud over and over and over again and so, I did. I repeated it until I believed it. I had already been writing in my journal every day, sharing my thoughts, writing affirmations and songs. I initially thought that this was just some newfound hobby that I had picked up. However, it became something that I found myself wanting to do all the time. As I started to recognize and believe that there was more to this than just the occasional past-time of writing, I began stepping out of my comfort zone. When people would ask what do you do? I found myself boldly responding "I am a writer." And yet, I had never actually published anything. I was completely stepping out of my comfort zone by responding with that answer. The reality of my life at that time, I was a stay at home mom who in her free time anticipated writing something, anything when I had a quiet moment to myself. I would love when random thoughts would simply pop in my head and I would rush to find a pen and paper. Even today when I find old journals or random pieces of paper with things that I have written, I am amazed that I wrote it.

Another way that I found myself stepping out of my comfort zone is when I decided to share my gift with a select few people. There were a few people in my life that I felt secure enough to read some of the things that I had written. Their responses confirmed and validated that there was a little bit more than just putting the pen to paper. It solidified for me that my words had meaning. I felt as if my writing was more than just an enjoyable outlet for me to express myself, but my words carried some weight that made a difference to somebody else.

I remember going to an Open Mic night. I brought my journal with me that had some of the things that I had written. For some unknown reason there was this tugging I felt in my core to stand before a room of people that I didn't even know and read something that I had written. I was so nervous to the point that I thought that I would pass out. My stomach was in knots and I was saying to myself "you don't have to do this, no one is forcing you to go up there and read anything." However, something in me knew that it was necessary for me to do this. Needless to say, I challenged myself that night, and I did it. I stood in front of an audience and read something that I had actually written. The response was overwhelming. The people enjoyed the piece that I read. They literally wanted more, but I had barely made it through the first reading, and so I declined. I was so proud of myself in that moment, for taking another opportunity to step out of my comfort zone. That was another one of those moments in time where for me I was panicking on the inside, and no one knew it, but I had inspired someone else to share their gift because I was courageous enough to listen to the voice inside of me, propelling me forward.

The simplicity of that moment reminds me every time that when we hide ourselves, we are hiding our gift to the world. We are not walking in our divine purpose. We are allowing fear to take us away from what we are being called to do. The truth is that our bodies and mind were created to feel, but we are totally in control of how we handle or respond to those feelings. So, don't let a moment of uncomfortable nervous jitters prevent you from sharing your wonderful gift with the world. There will be moments of uncertainty, times when you will lack clarity, doubt will creep into your mind, playing tricks on your confidence but that is just part of the process.

The thought behind sharing these different specific "right now" moments, is to make you aware that the more you walk in your gift, the more real it becomes for you and others. It becomes more energized because it is being exercised. Your willingness to enter a room and enact by its very presence is a step in the right direction.

I clearly believe that writing this book as well as the others that will follow, that I am being used to be a catalyst that sparks and provokes thought in the minds of all who are on the journey of discovering their purpose, walking in their purpose, and living their purpose.

"The lyric must never let go of the listener for a single instant. It's like fishing, a little slack in the line and they're off the hook." (Oscar Hammerstein II 1895-1960)

When I first read this quote, I immediately thought of the words that I write. My hope is that each and every sentence, idea, and shared thought is influential in making a change in the life of you, the reader. No matter how small or big, that it lights a fire in your soul. My hope is that my words cause someone's thoughts to be elevated and moved to manifestation. I want my words to be the motivation that is used to propel some action from you, the reader, to influence the impact that each of you will make on the world. That is my ultimate goal.

When a singer writes/ performs/ shares a song with us the listener, he/she is singing from a very personal, individual place, but somehow millions of us listeners hear and feel that same energy all across the world. We are touched by just one person's willingness to share a piece of themselves.

My point in sharing is to acknowledge that we all are individuals who carry a gift that can reach multitudes of people. If we just tap into what that is, the Universe itself will begin to rejoice in response to our obedience and join us in creating movement towards that fulfillment.

The discovery of purpose leads to a sense of inner peace that creates a resounding happiness that radiates through us, touching other people. The discovery of purpose provides meaning and gives way to the light that shines within us. It not only creates energy but manifests itself as energy. I know for me, the more that I engage in writing, the more content and satisfied I am on the inside, that I am moving towards a successful end.

Of course, some of you reading this already have a clear idea of what your purpose in life is, but the struggle may be navigating your way through obstacles and distractions. I am a witness that it can be challenging. I suffered from knowing what I was passionate about but not knowing how I could or should I say how I would align my passion with my purpose. Eventually I realized all I needed to do was just start somewhere, anywhere. As all of you readers witness the unwrapping of my gift,

I'd like to encourage all of you to simply get started, go for it!! You have absolutely nothing to lose.

My intent is to be completely transparent as I journey through this writing adventure. I am not the writer who had an outline, nor did I have things broken down by chapters. I just began to write. However, having an outline and creating specific chapters may be a great idea if you find that writing is your purpose. I would also like to add that all of you may not feel an overwhelming sensational feeling that you are operating in your purpose. I certainly did not. I did recognize that I really enjoyed putting words to paper and I enjoyed the responses of those who read what I wrote. I did not realize how significant or impactful my words were. But that was my purpose. Not every purpose has this mystical moment or requires some huge task.

For me what would often happen is that I would post positive daily affirmations on social media. I would get several likes. It wasn't until one day I decided that I would take a hiatus away from social media, and I included that as one of my post. I received an overwhelming amount of inboxes and messages, asking why was I leaving social media. People began to express that they looked forward to my positive post every morning when they woke up. Those sentiments really took me by surprise. My purpose was just to share my positive thoughts to counteract all of the negativity that people experience and read on social media. This was confirmation for me. The simple fact that I was just writing a daily post to keep people encouraged, was making a difference in the lives of others on a smaller scale. There is no act too small that can be done to make an impact on the lives of others.

Discovery, the action or process of finding, locating, uncovering, unearthing, recognizing, and realizing something that was unknown...

Sometimes the discovery of your **purpose** is born out of adversity. This reminds me of the scripture Romans 8:28, "And we know that **all things work together** for good to them that love God, to them who are the called according to his purpose (KJV)," as well as the song *Intentional* by Travis Greene. I am able to clearly see that all things are working for my good, because God is intentional about every area of our lives. Because of our imperfections, and our mistakes, God is able to show up and demonstrate His divine power in our lives. Those seemingly uncomfortable moments that we experience are oftentimes the very events that lead us straight to our divine **purpose.** The Lord allows us to be the example, the witnesses, and the testimony, so that others won't feel as though they are alone in the challenges that they may be going through. It is so important that we understand who we are and who our Father is. Knowing this without a shadow of doubt, gives us the boldness and the confidence that we need to be effective in completing our God given assignment.

False Evidence Appearing Real

As I set about the process of discovering my purpose, I began to reflect on the many fear-based thoughts I had that were causing my procrastination in moving towards and walking in my purpose. After doing some research on fear and what it means, I found that fear was clearly a weapon being used against us to attack our minds and attempt to delay our blessings. The intention of fear is to paralyze us in such a way that we are unable to share with others what God has given us to deliver. Fear serves as a distractor that takes us away from our purpose. It creates in us self-doubt and requires us to try to hide who we are and what we are being charged to do. Fear, when allowed to grow, will hinder us from walking in our purpose, prevent us from fulfilling our divine destiny, and taint our journey towards peace, happiness, and fulfillment.

Ask yourself, do you want fear to be the reason why your purpose is not being fulfilled? I asked myself that very question, and I decided that I would rather answer the call, instead of living with any regrets of not trying at all. The fact is that we all have a job to do, and it is for the uplifting of the Kingdom of God. I personally don't want to leave this earth not having completed the task that was specifically assigned to me.

Another truth is that we are all "one of a kind" and no other human being on this earth can do what was ordained for us to do. When you feel that persistent tugging at your soul about the same thing over and over and over again, that is God's amazing grace and mercy tapping you on your shoulder reminding and confirming that you have something on the inside of you that is trying to breakthrough to the outside of you, to do what it has been purposed to do. When you finally discover what that thing is, you have to give it life. You have to take the first step, make the first call, write the first line. We have been deceived long enough and it is time to be witnesses to God's greatness. You can't allow fear control your answer to the call. Truthfully, there will come a point when the call is so loud it can't be ignored, the itch so strong, the only way to soothe it is to scratch. And so, it becomes that the fear becomes but a whispering voice, drowned out by the fulfillment of your purpose.

In your process of discovery, you will find that there are many things that you really enjoy doing and that you are really good at doing. It could be that your talents may work jointly together, or you are simply a multi-talented person. The gift that is designed to build the Kingdom of God and enrich the souls that experience it, will be anointed, and set apart in such a way, that you will not be able to deny it. The gift that is designed for **Purpose** is longing for the opportunity to serve at all times. Your ability to differentiate will solely depend on how well you focus and are in tune with what is authentic in you. What I have learned for sure is that you have to believe in your gift, and trust that God will give you direction to execute it to its fullest potential. In doing so, fear is replaced with confidence and peace.

When you finally discover what that thing is, you have to give it life. You have to take the first step, make the first call, write the first line, to let fear know that you are no longer going to let it win. We have been deceived long enough and it is time to be witnesses to God's greatness.

"Now FAITH is the substance of things hoped for, the evidence of things not seen."

Hebrews 11:1 (KJV)

It requires Faith to be able to access the promises that God has declared over us. "I am convinced that the currency of Faith is the confession of my mouth." When I heard John Gray the Associate Pastor at Lakewood Church in Houston, Texas, say that quote, it struck a chord in me. I am aware that the distance between where we are now and where we are going is our Faith walk. Every step that I take is taking me somewhere.

A Faith walk will require a Faith plan. A measurable course of action, incremental steps, maximizing my ability to get from one place to the next. I know that all of that sounds well and good, however sometimes we don't always have that plan written out, or in our thoughts. In my experience exercising my faith, especially in writing this book, it has been scary. I have felt feelings of not being qualified enough to write this book. I've wondered if people will even be interested in what I have to say about this subject. Even though I have had moments of doubt and what feels like fear, it has not deterred me from getting the task complete. My faith has certainly been challenged.

I realized that my obedience plus my trust in God is the sum of my faith. Trust takes work and vulnerability, and obedience requires submission. In writing this book I have been able to explore my fears. I acknowledge that I was very comfortable being the person that worked behind the scenes. I can assist anybody with anything and not require any accolades or recognition. In this moment I can't hide the fact that I am being pushed to the forefront and demonstrating my willingness to let go of my fears.

God has shown himself strong in many other areas in my life, which made it simple for me to surrender. I am confident that writing this book was assigned to me, or else I would not be stressing out to get it finished. My point is that this is what faith looks like for me, I took the first step in putting pen to the paper and that was all the activation that I needed to get the ball rolling. For you, I am not exactly sure of what it will take, but just know that if you feel a little fear or doubt, simply take the next step and see what happens on the other side.

It is faith that overcomes fear. By choosing to be obedient, to trust, and to believe, I am no longer a slave to the fear that prevents me from fulfilling my purpose. I acknowledge my fear but I do not allow it to be the distraction that prevents me from walking in God's divine purpose or using my gifts for the benefit of others. It is the very presence of faith that makes fear shutter. Do you dare to take this walk with me?

I am optimistic about my unknown journey ahead to inspire other people through the POWER of my words. This statement is really what I believe the core of what God has **purposed** for my life, to serve the Kingdom of God.

It is 4:41a.m., it is still dark outside, my eyes are barely open. I realize that today is the day. The date is September 29, 2017, the last day that I report to my current job. I begin my regular morning prayer, thanking God for waking me up, acknowledging God for who HE is. I began to say ok God we have arrived, the day is here. I felt this awkward feeling in the pit of my stomach that if it could speak words, it would say...OMG!!!! What am

I doing? How am I supposed to continue to take care of my bills and responsibilities with no job? Yes, I said "no job". On September 7, 2017, I resigned from my job knowing that I had a greater purpose to fulfill. I figured either I am losing my mind, or I am seriously taking a huge leap of Faith. "God, I am trying to follow your lead, and I haven't heard you say apply for a particular job", not to mention the fact that my lease is up at the end of this month and I was thinking that I don't want to pay another $1200.00 for rent. I am talking to God saying, "is this smart?"

I clearly remember the day that I had the thought to resign from my job. It was August and I was in the midst of a month long spiritual fast and I thought to myself maybe I am just excited and so full of the presence of God that I am just having a moment of wanting to please God in every way. Initially, I didn't say anything to anyone, but it continued to weigh heavily on my conscience, so I decided to share my thoughts with two others that were participating in the spiritual fast with me. I was clearly seeking some feedback that possibly made sense to me. The feedback that I received from one friend was, "alright, I am so excited to see what God is going to do." The response from the other was "Do you have a backup plan?" "Have you applied for other jobs?" "God operates in decency and in order." These responses caused me to question what I knew I heard in my spirit.

My thoughts immediately were God I need some clarity and direction. God, I want to be obedient. I knew that I had never ever considered anything like this in my entire 47 years of living. At this point, I have asked God to send me confirmations every day in every possible way. I was absolutely certain that I was in a transitional place in every possible area of my life. I had a clear understanding that I was being propelled forward, being pushed in a new direction. I was being challenged to do something different in my life. What was churning inside of me was not born out of a desire or want but a need to do something different with my life, to move towards my purpose, to answer the voice that was calling deep in my soul.

Many months before, I had spoken into the Universe that I wanted to live a more purposeful life. I wanted to be proactive about making a difference in the lives of others. Be careful of what you ask for, because sometimes, most times, when you least expect it, you will get that knock on the door. That whispering voice in your spirit gets louder and louder until the only way you can silence it is to begin to move. You can't avoid the tug. The Universe will make you uncomfortable and challenge you to take the first step. You might even, at times question your sanity as I did but no matter the doubts that creep in, the fear that tries to bubble, that voice speaks louder, you find the courage to take flight.

Visualizing My Thoughts

There I sat one day, glancing at my vision board, and I was reminded of everything that I wanted to fulfill, the words I had spoken aloud to the Universe.

So here is the vision board that sits directly in my view every morning when I open my eyes. This is actually the same vision board that I created in 2015 with the exception of changing the five into a six and then into a seven. I realized that I wanted to achieve all of the goals that I set for myself that are mentioned on the board. I also realized that I was not doing anything specific or noteworthy to accomplish those goals either. In our hearts and minds there are so many things that we truly want to accomplish, but everyday life events somehow zap the excitement of that initial energy to make those changes.

What I do know for sure is that timing is everything. When things begin to **align** in your life starting with your commitment to what it is that you want to do, and the energy that you follow up with to complete it, it causes the Universe to respond to the atmosphere that you are creating. And so, it is the old saying, "faith without works is dead." To accomplish the things on my vision board, to begin to live my life in the way that I desired, to be able to make an impact on the world I had to take bold, daring steps. I had to move out of my comfort zone. I asked God, He spoke to me, and all that was being required of me now was obedience and trust.

In all actuality, this vision board was the blueprint to the life that I am finally stepping into today. I am literally fulfilling some of the very things that you see on the vision board. My hope is to **change the world** with my writing. As you are witnessing, I am actually **writing the book** which I started in January **2017**. I honestly feel that I am creating an ambiance of **purposeful living** and it is **manifesting** through my **Faith** and my **Hope** and my **Belief**. I am living a life Free to do what I believe will **Elevate** the lives of others as well as my own. I believe that this **gift of now** will allow me the opportunities to **travel**, to have increase and abundance, to have my wants and wishes and fulfill my Journey to happy. This act of Faith has created **Balance** in me that allows me to exercise **mindfulness** as well as exercise my physical body and nourish my spiritual being. There is a **Peace** that comes along with operating in your God given **Purpose** that cannot be explained but only EXPERIENCED. There is **Power** in your **Passion** to pursue your **Purpose**.

Mission Statement

We are all on a mission whether we know what that is or not. According to the google dictionary, Mission is defined as an important assignment, or commission, or journey. It is often looked at as a vocation or calling, a goal, a quest, last but not least a Purpose that needs to be carried out. When we think of large or small corporations or businesses, we often notice that they have what is called a "Mission Statement" on which they stand by and use to guide them. It may be located on a wall or printed in a handbook, however, it describes who they are and what they represent and desire to accomplish with what service they provide. On our journey we will find that having a mission and creating a mission statement will bring focus to the road that is set before us. In this right now moment, here is an opportunity for you to dig deep and give thought to what you believe your mission in this life is destined to be.

I Am...

What is it that you do that makes you feel alive? Is it something that you would do without even getting paid for it? If your answer is yes, you are definitely on the right path to discovering your divine **purpose.**

I asked a few friends if they would be interested in sharing with the world how they came to discover what their **purpose** was and to give me some insight to share with you all about how they discovered their divine reason for living and this is what they had to say:

Deborah

At the age of 25, standing in my living room vacuuming, God's Spirit moved on me and I began to sing "I Come to the Garden Alone" crying. My hands went up and the vacuum cleaner fell to the floor. God from that point on, began to draw me closer, teaching me to worship Him. I am a worshiper and a Psalmist. At the age of 27, while standing in church, worshipping, God's Spirit moved on me, I began to speak in a new tongue. I had spoken in unknown tongues as early as the age of 9, having my first Pentecostal experience, however this was different. It was not with stammering lips, it was a tongue that spoke clearly in a language that I did not speak, however, He interpreted it for me telling me, "Feed My Sheep." I knew that I was called to minister to His people. He later expanded my understanding, telling me I was His Ambassador. In my early 30's feeling the weight of the callings on my life, one day while feeling sorry for myself, kneeling in my den, crying and praying, I heard the sound of chimes, startled, I looked up and saw an angel. He came to tell me how much God loves me, and I was to get up and go tell others. He defined my mission as God's Ambassadors. Lastly, when I was considering divorcing my husband at the age of 36, God moved on me again, while standing in church, worshipping. He said to me, "Give me your heart." He promised to heal and restore my heart. He renewed the love between my husband and I, told me some years later to return to school, to become a Marriage and Family counselor.

Victoria

Hey I hope I'm not too late....when did I discover what my purpose was? It was when I began to do it naturally without any effort. I couldn't stop thinking about it, I woke up and went to sleep thinking about it. I would have dreams about it as well. I really knew what my purpose was when people were being blessed by it.

Believe it or not it took me until a few years ago to really figure out what my true purpose was. I mean I've been singing all my life. It was something that I really could do in my sleep. But to actually minister through song beyond the notes and the lyrics was something different. I didn't want to punch another person's clock because I felt like that was wasted time that I could be using to push my purpose. I knew I wanted to sing but I didn't know that I wanted to do ministry. It's like I got bit by the bug or purpose.

Now I approach what I do differently. It's my baby and I protect it at all cost. I have to live my purpose out until the day I die. There are lives at stake. I can't afford to allow what God had given, to go undone.

Nasha

Hi Carmen! I'll never forget our unfinished intro convo (my fault) but I'll always remember you finishing what you started! Way to go!

My purpose is to function as a connector. I was in my mid to late 20's when I could articulate this because of the kind of student I was in college. I recognized that I can naturally make connections between academic disciplines and relationships between ideas and resources, including people, that helped facilitate understanding and created opportunities. As a student, making connections helped me excel as a scholar and success has momentum. For example, earning A's led to more A's, campus and community involvement led to deeper engagement and scholarships from this activity attracted more scholarships. This led me to reflect on common threads of behaviors and activities throughout my youth that highlighted how this purpose reveals itself.

There was a point during my first semester in community college when my intention shifted. I opted out of higher education for 3 years until I recognized needing a degree to get a better job.

There were a few experiences in engaging with coursework where I pivoted from being career oriented to mission oriented - from something passive and required to feeling pulled and attracted. The level of intrinsic motivation, unrelenting interest, and growing passion propelled my academic performance and I excelled in school in a way that I never had before.

Andrea

As you know, I was diagnosed with cancer back in 2009. I knew from that experience that I was to do something that would be great. When I say great, I'm meaning impactful. At that point, I wasn't sure exactly what it was but I thought it would have something to do with breast cancer and the African American community. But just 1 year later, I was battling another cancer so I thought maybe my scope was too small. I should deal with AA and cancer.

It was during this time that I went to Case to get my executive coaching certification. One of the exercises that I had to do made me look at the things I love to do, the strengths that I possess, my skills, my experiences, and my heart. I had a one-on-one with a coach and I realized that the theme around all that I loved was to help live the life they desired and loved. I love helping people make their dreams come true. I had done it previously when I was in real estate and was currently doing it by coaching people. I started spending two hours each day on personal development and learning more about me. I looked inside myself and starting paying attention to how I lived my life and how it affected others.

I realized that I had a gift of gravitas. Someone told me that once and I had to look it up. But once I read it, I understood what he was saying. I have a way of getting people to trust me and respect me and what I say.

When asked what my purpose is, I say, "To open hearts, blossom compassion (and passion) and to help inspire people to live their lives...on purpose. Meaning with intention.

Cancer led me to my purpose and I'm grateful for that. The lens that I see the world through is so different, so much clearer. I consider my cancer experience a blessing.

I am passionate about what I'm called to do. I believe that passion and purpose go hand-in-hand with one another. They are partners. I believe your passion leads you into your purpose.

I know that this is my purpose because it's what made my soul alive. It stirs my soul. It awakens me.

As you have read, the arrival to our God given purpose is uniquely tailored for every individual. No two experiences are ever the same. We all have a story to tell with our lives. There is an audience of people eagerly awaiting your testimony to help them along their life's journey. We are all fitly joined together in one way or another to build a community that serves one another to reach our highest potential.

My assignment was to literally write this book. Assignment complete!

Your assignment is to tap into what it is that you already know is tugging at your soul, it is probably tugging right now, in this moment as you are reading this, and now it is your responsibility to take the first step, hear the voice, and do something about it.

"We all have to be willing to proceed in our individuality, our self-mastery, our uniqueness."-unknown

When I arose this morning at 5:09 a.m., my first thought was God thank you for waking me up again. My very next thought was, I am going to get my journal and begin to write a prayer to God to express to Him what I was feeling. Before I could begin the prayer, I was fumbling through to the next available empty page in the journal, and I found a scrap piece of paper in my handwriting with the quote, "we all have to be willing to proceed in our individuality, our self-mastery, our uniqueness." There was no name that followed the quote. However, after reading that I was led to read the very last entry that I had written in this particular journal:

Sunday, January 22, 2017
Ok! So today is a very exciting day for me, because I have decided that there will be no more procrastinating. The book, The Gift of Now is being written (worked on) RIGHT NOW!

It has been revealed to me that my title has more than one meaning... it means living and cherishing and being in every moment of "NOW" as well as using your "GIFT" now in this moment, the time is "Now" and all you have to do is show up.

When I first heard the phrase "show up", it resonated with my spirit. It was clear that all I needed to do was be present in whatever moment that I was in. The times when I didn't think that my presence was necessary, someone would always come with kind words and affirm otherwise. Those encounters confirm that it really doesn't matter what we feel like to ourselves, the point is that we really have so much to offer just by showing up when asked.

This reminds me of what I heard from my elders who are much wiser than me, "there is something much bigger than us, a work that needs to be completed, and we have to keep our eyes focused on the big picture." We all suffer from conflicts within. The fact that we are still present is the very witness that we need to know that we can make it through any obstacle. We are resilient, and that is evidenced by the fact that we keep showing up.

Thank you for going on this journey with me. I am living proof of what simply being obedient and responding to that tugging in my tummy looks like. It just wouldn't leave me alone until I made it to where I am right in this moment...Finished with this book!!!

Who got next?

Questions to ask yourself:

- ♥ What is it that you would love to do with your life?
- ♥ What do you enjoy doing in your free time?
- ♥ What are you good at?
- ♥ What is something that you have wanted to do but haven't done yet?
- ♥ What is your mission statement?

Be curious and courageous in your quest, take some time and give yourself a moment to discover the things that will make your soul smile!

Acknowledgments

I would like to Humbly Acknowledge my mother Joann (RIP), for giving birth to me; my dad Ronald Hall for teaching me to be responsible for my own actions, and that there are consequences to every chosen behavior; my stepmom Valeria, for being the best example of a "step-parent", that I have ever witnessed; my brother Ronald (Mokey) Hall, for being the ultimate supportive big brother through all of my life events; my sister's Anissa and Ariane for making me feel proud to be their big sister; my 5 beautiful gifts, my children Jordan, Morgan self - proclaimed "Daughterger", Micah (my future accountant), Camren (Endless encouragement), and last but not least Jadan (my mini me), for teaching me humility and selflessness...and we must not forget the granddaughter Ava Ca'ryn.

I would like to express my profound gratitude to those who helped me directly with bringing the vision of writing and completing this book to fruition; Beyond Wynn for your continued inspiration and demonstration of greatness every day that you wake up; Andrea D. Campbell, for sharing your story and your testimony of faith as well as your knowledge with me; Michelle King-Lewis for blessing me with your gift of editing, you are an amazing gift and a life saver; Tracy D. Zalit Davidson for being an incredible communicator of words that provoked me to ask you to write my foreword; Jermalle Stephens (early stages) and Christopher Cyrus (finished product) for assisting me with bringing my cover to life. Thank you all so much for giving freely of your time, hearts, resources and support.

To the host of close family (Ikieya Wynn) and friends (Kelly Anderson & The Girls) who have shown me *tremendous love and support when I clearly felt that I did not know what I was doing with my life. You all are the reason that the procrastination had to end and the writing had to begin. I thank each and every one of you for believing in the gift that God assigned specifically to me.*

A very special thank you to Victoria, Deborah, Andrea and Nasha for allowing me to share the beautiful experience of the discovery of your Purpose with the world.